CHAMPAGNE
COCKTAILS

Special thanks to Moét-Hennessy USA for providing product for recipe development and the photography. And thanks to TMD Liqueurs (www.tmdliqueurs.com) for providing their award-winning Passionfruit Liqueur for the photography.

This book is printed on acid-free paper.

Published by John Wiley & Sons, Inc., Hoboken, New Jersey
Published simultaneously in Canada

Book design by Elizabeth Van Itallie
Food styling by Mindy Fox
Prop styling by Leslie Siegel

Library of Congress Cataloging-in-Publication Data:

Haasarud, Kim.
  101 champagne cocktails / Kim Haasarud ; photography by Alexandra Grablewski.
     p. cm.
  Includes index.
  ISBN 978-0-470-16942-1 (cloth)
  1. Cocktails. 2. Champagne (Wine) I. Title. II. Title: One hundred one champagne cocktails. III. Title: One hundred and one champagne cocktails.
  TX951.H185 2008
  641.8'74--dc22

                          2007041608

Printed in China

10 9 8 7 6 5 4 3 2 1

CHAMPAGNE COCKTAILS

KIM HAASARUD

Photography by Alexandra Grablewski

JOHN WILEY & SONS, INC.

THE ULTIMATE CELEBRATION LIBATION

Champagne and her sparkling-wine sisters are renowned the world over as the grand dames of celebration. Corks popping, frothy liquid flowing, a cold crispy freshness . . . nothing quite so perfectly reflects the notion of "the best in life." Classic champagnes like Dom Pérignon, Veuve Clicquot, and Taittinger, as well as regional sparklers like Italy's spumante, Spain's Cava, Alsace's Crémant, and Napa's sparkling wine—all are part of the worldwide bounty.

Bubbly has presided over weddings, births, the coronation of kings, the launching of ships, and treaty signings between nations. Louis XIV drank it exclusively. The self-appointed emperor Napoléon Bonaparte would swing his army through the Champagne region of France, claiming "In victory you deserve it, in defeat you need it."

Champagne cocktails have likely been around as long as the sparkling wine itself. It is not hard to imagine Dom Pierre Pérignon and his monks throwing a little fresh fruit into their glasses to add some seasonal freshness. Go to any self-respecting watering hole today, and you will find an array of sparkling wine–based goodness. As with all cocktails, using the freshest ingredients and a decent base is the recipe for success.

This is a book for celebrants. It is a book for romantics. It is a book for the entertainer who wants a light, fresh concoction that can bring people together to accent the joys of the day. So break out the bubbly and toast!

CHAMPAGNE VS. SPARKLING WINE

By definition, real champagne must come from the Champagne region of France. However, it is commonplace to use the term *champagne* to mean all types of sparkling wine. Throughout this book, I use the term *champagne* loosely to include all sparkling wines. However, I do make note of some specific brands and types of sparkling wine that I feel are most appropriate for a specific cocktail. This book really runs the gamut with all types of sparkling wines in all price ranges. So, if you're feeling really decadent and are toasting a special occasion, break out the good stuff. If you're having a party and are on a budget, go for the off-the-rack, $10 sparkling wines; there are some great ones on the market.

PUREES

Various fruit purees are used throughout the book, especially in the Bellini section (page 38). If the fruit is in season, I highly recommend making your own. (See some recipes on pages 7–9.) To make a fruit puree, simply cut and peel fruit (if applicable) and blend with a small amount of simple syrup (recipe below) until smooth. The purees can be frozen and kept for several months. If the fruit is not in season, there are some great puree companies whose products I recommend. They flash freeze their purees, keeping them as fresh tasting as possible. Here are a few:

Perfect Puree. This is a company based in California with a huge selection of purees. They can be purchased online (and even on Amazon.com), and they ship worldwide. For information, see www.perfectpuree.com.

Boiron. This is a puree company based in France. While their selection is not as big as some others, their purees are of excellent and superior quality. They also have some interesting puree blends made with harder-to-find fruits and spices. They can often be found at gourmet or chef stores. For information, see www.boironfreres.com.

Funkin' Fruit. These makers are based in the United Kingdom but distribute here in the United States. Their packaging is bartender-friendly and their purees very tasty. For information, see www.funkin.us.

PEACH PUREE

Makes approximately 2 cups

5 WHITE PEACHES, RIPE
SIMPLE SYRUP (PAGE 9), IF NEEDED

Fill a saucepan with water and heat until boiling. Add the peaches, and cook briefly (blanch) for 1 to 2 minutes to help loosen the skin. Transfer the peaches to a bowl of cool water. Once cool, remove the skin and slice the fruit. Place sliced peaches in a blender and blend until smooth. If needed, add a bit of simple syrup to sweeten the puree. Use immediately or freeze for later.

RASPBERRY PUREE

*Makes ³/₄ cup or approximately enough for 6 cocktail
servings*

2 PINTS RASPBERRIES, RINSED
1 TO 2 OUNCES SIMPLE SYRUP (SEE OPPOSITE)

Place the raspberries in a blender. Add 1 ounce of
simple syrup, and blend until smooth. If the
puree is extremely thick, add more simple syrup
until smooth and pourable.

About Raw Eggs
Raw eggs are used in many cocktails as a
textural element; it can add a bit of froth,
foam, and creaminess to a cocktail that is
hard to duplicate using any other ingredient. Many people are nervous about using
raw eggs for fear of getting *Salmonella
enteridis* or other foodborne bacteria; but
the risk is minimal if mixing the eggs with
alcohol, which kills the bacteria. However,
the FDA recommends using eggs that have
been treated to destroy *Salmonella* or pasteurized egg products. And, while crack-
ing open an egg and dropping it into a
cocktail shaker makes for a great perform-
ance, pasteurized egg whites and yolks
work just as well.

SIMPLE SYRUP

This simple mixture of sugar and water in equal parts is a base ingredient for many cocktails. Make some in advance; it can be stored in your refrigerator for weeks.

½ CUP SUGAR
½ CUP HOT WATER

In a small bowl, glass, or empty, clean wine bottle, combine the sugar with the hot water and stir, or shake bottle, until sugar is completely dissolved. Let cool completely before using.

FRESH SOUR

Makes 1 cup (or 8 ounces)

This recipe is used as a sweet-and-sour element in many recipes. While you can buy a sour mix at any grocery store, it won't be as good as the kind you make yourself using fresh lemon and lime juice. Squeeze the fruit juice immediately before using for optimum freshness.

¼ CUP FRESHLY SQUEEZED LIME JUICE
   (APPROXIMATELY 2 MEDIUM LIMES)
¼ CUP FRESHLY SQUEEZED LEMON JUICE
   (APPROXIMATELY 1½ LEMONS)
½ CUP SIMPLE SYRUP (SEE ABOVE)

In a small bowl, glass, or empty, clean wine bottle, combine all the ingredients. Stir, or shake bottle, to combine; cover and keep refrigerated until ready to use.

I

CLASSIC CHAMPAGNE COCKTAIL

The champagne shines through in this classic—with a hint of added flavor from spirits, bitters, and citrus peels. Many variations of this recipe are served at hotels and bars worldwide.

1 SUGAR CUBE
ANGOSTURA BITTERS
CHAMPAGNE
LEMON OR ORANGE TWIST, FOR GARNISH

Soak the sugar cube in Angostura bitters and drop into a champagne flute. Top with a luxury champagne or a sparkling wine. Garnish with a lemon or orange twist.

2

MODERN CHAMPAGNE COCKTAIL

Instead of Angostura bitters, use Stirrings Blood Orange bitters and a long orange twist. (Available online at www.stirrings.com.)

TIP: *Sugar often revitalizes the bubbles in champagne. If you have an open bottle of bubbly in the refrigerator that has lost its fizz, add a sugar cube!*

3

CHAMPAGNE CELEBRATION

This cocktail debuted in Las Vegas on the Bellagio hotel's first holiday menu and should accompany the toast, "To good health, good fortune, and infinite happiness!" Created by Tony Abou-Ganim, the Modern Mixologist.

1 SUGAR CUBE
PEYCHAUD'S BITTERS
½ OUNCE HENNESSY VSOP COGNAC
½ OUNCE COINTREAU
CHILLED MOËT & CHANDON WHITE STAR
   CHAMPAGNE
LONG ORANGE TWIST, FOR GARNISH

Soak the sugar cube in Peychaud's bitters and drop into a champagne flute. Add the cognac and Cointreau. Slowly fill with champagne and garnish with long orange twist.

TIP: *Chill the Hennessy and Cointreau in the refrigerator before mixing the drink.*

Bayou Champagne Cocktail

Another variation on the classic champagne cocktail, but made with Peychaud's bitters and Southern Comfort, two spirits native to New Orleans.

1 SUGAR CUBE
ANGOSTURA BITTERS
PEYCHAUD'S BITTERS
½ OUNCE SOUTHERN COMFORT
CHAMPAGNE
ORANGE TWIST, FOR GARNISH

Add 2 dashes each of the Angostura and Peychaud's bitters to the sugar cube and drop into a champagne flute. Add the Southern Comfort, and slowly pour champagne into the flute. Garnish with orange twist.

4

Ritz Cocktail

This cocktail, now a classic, was created in the 1980s by Dale DeGroff, master mixologist and author of The Craft of the Cocktail *(New York: Clarkson Potter, 2002). It was inspired by some of the signature hotel champagne cocktails.*

1 OUNCE REMY MARTIN cognac
½ OUNCE COINTREAU
½ OUNCE maraschino liqueur
½ OUNCE fresh lemon juice
MOËT & CHANDON White Star champagne
LARGE ORANGE PEEL, FOR GARNISH

In a mixing glass, stir the cognac, Cointreau, maraschino liqueur, and lemon juice together with ice. Strain into a cocktail glass and fill with champagne. Hold the orange peel over the glass (skin side down) and over a flame from a match or lighter. Carefully squeeze into the flame so that the oils from the orange peel pass through the flame and into the drink. Drop the peel into the drink and serve.

5

6
Italian Champagne Cocktail

1 OUNCE BLOOD ORANGE JUICE (OR PUREE)
½ OUNCE CAMPARI (OR APEROL, FOR A LESS
   BITTER COCKTAIL)
PROSECCO (AN ITALIAN SPARKLING WINE)
BLOOD ORANGE HALF WHEEL, FOR GARNISH

Combine the blood orange juice and Campari in a cocktail shaker with ice. Shake moderately and strain into a champagne flute. Drop in blood orange half-wheel and fill with chilled Prosecco.

Oscar 78

I created this cocktail for a Rolling Stone *magazine party for the 78th Annual Academy Awards.*

1 TABLESPOON PEAR PUREE (SEE RECIPE
   BELOW, OR BUY FROM PERFECTPUREE.COM)
1 ½ OUNCE PEAR LIQUEUR
1 OUNCE RUM SYRUP (SEE RECIPE BELOW)
½ OUNCE FRESH LEMON JUICE
1 ½ OUNCE PREMIUM VODKA
1 OUNCE CHAMPAGNE
THIN SLICE OF PEAR, FOR GARNISH

In a cocktail shaker, combine the puree, syrup, lemon juice, and vodka with ice. Shake vigorously and strain into martini glass. Top off with champagne. Garnish with thin slice of pear.

Pear puree: Core and slice 4 pears. (Use Bosc pears, if ripe.) Sauté in a small pan with 4 tablespoons simple syrup (see page 9) until the pears are softened. Add 1 ½ ounces of a pear liqueur, and stir for another minute. Remove from the heat and let cool. Puree in a blender until smooth and set aside.

Rum syrup: Combine 1 part dark rum with 1 part sugar in a saucepan over low heat. Stir until the sugar is completely dissolved and the mixture is translucent. Let cool and set aside.

7

8
FRENCH 75

Named after the famous French World War I artillery gun, the 75 mm howitzer, also called a "French 75," this is a great cocktail for hot summer months. There are several different recipes for this cocktail floating around (some of which use cognac or brandy in lieu of gin); but this one, which is a little lighter on the lemon juice, is my favorite.

1 OUNCE GIN (PLYMOUTH IS A GOOD CHOICE)
½ OUNCE FRESH LEMON JUICE
½ OUNCE SIMPLE SYRUP (SEE PAGE 9)
CHAMPAGNE
LEMON TWIST, FOR GARNISH

Combine the gin, lemon juice, and simple syrup in a cocktail shaker with ice. Shake vigorously and strain into a champagne flute. Top off with champagne and garnish with lemon peel.

Passionate French 75

½ OUNCE PASSIONFRUIT PUREE (OR NECTAR,
   FOUND AT MOST GROCERY STORES)
½ OUNCE NAVAN VANILLA LIQUEUR
½ OUNCE SIMPLE SYRUP (SEE PAGE 9)
MOËT & CHANDON WHITE STAR CHAMPAGNE
GRATED LEMON ZEST AND MINT SPRIG FOR
   GARNISH

Combine the passionfruit puree, vanilla liqueur,
and simple syrup in a cocktail shaker with ice.
Shake vigorously and strain into a champagne
flute. Top with champagne. (Or serve over ice in a
highball glass.) Top with Moët & Chandon White
Star champagne. Garnish with lemon zest and a
mint sprig.

10
PASSION ROUGE

*Created by master mixologist Francesco LaFranconi—
one of his favorite champagne cocktails to date.
Francesco is the director of mixology for Southern Wine
& Spirits of America.*

1 OUNCE GRAND MARNIER
1 OUNCE PASSIONFRUIT LIQUEUR (PASSOA)
¾ OUNCE PASSIONFRUIT PUREE
¾ OUNCE ORANGE JUICE
2 DASHES ANGOSTURA BITTERS
½ OUNCE PASTEURIZED EGG WHITE (THIS WILL
   GIVE THE COCKTAIL A NICE FOAMY LOOK AND
   TEXTURE)
CHAMPAGNE
ORANGE TWIST, FOR GARNISH
GROUND NUTMEG, FOR GARNISH

Combine the Grand Marnier, passionfruit
liqueur, passionfruit puree, orange juice, bitters,
and egg white in a cocktail shaker with ice. Shake
vigorously for 10 seconds. Add about an ounce of
champagne to the mix and stir. Strain into a martini glass. Garnish with orange twist and a sprinkle
of nutmeg.

11
ROYAL GIN FIZZ

1 OUNCE GIN
½ OUNCE CRÈME DE CASSIS
1 EGG WHITE (OR 1 TABLESPOON PASTEURIZED
   EGG WHITE)
½ OUNCE SIMPLE SYRUP (SEE PAGE 9)
3 OUNCES CHAMPAGNE
3 TO 4 BLACKBERRIES, FOR GARNISH
   (OPTIONAL)

Combine the gin, crème de cassis, egg white, and
simple syrup in a cocktail shaker with ice. Shake
vigorously for 10 seconds. Add the champagne and
stir for 5 seconds. Strain into a highball glass filled
with ice. If desired, garnish with blackberries.

12
PERUVIAN APRICOT FIZZ

1 ½ OUNCES PISCO BRANDY
1 ½ OUNCES APRICOT NECTAR
1 ½ OUNCES PINEAPPLE JUICE
½ OUNCE TRIPLE SEC
SPLASH OF SIMPLE SYRUP (SEE PAGE 9)
1 ½ OUNCES CHAMPAGNE

Combine the brandy, apricot nectar, pineapple
juice, triple sec, and simple syrup in a cocktail
shaker with ice. Shake vigorously and strain into a
cocktail glass. Top off with champagne.

SUNNYSIDE PICK-ME-UP

Inspired by the classic cocktail "Cecil Pick-Me-Up,"
this flip is sure to help with a hangover, giving a little
kick of protein. (See "About Raw Eggs" page 8.)

1 SMALL EGG YOLK (OR 1 TABLESPOON
   PASTEURIZED EGG YOLK)
1 OUNCE BRANDY (OR COGNAC)
½ OUNCE ORANGE CURAÇAO
½ OUNCE SIMPLE SYRUP (SEE PAGE 9)
½ OUNCE HALF & HALF (OR LIGHT CREAM)
3 TO 4 OUNCES CHAMPAGNE
ORANGE TWIST, FOR GARNISH

Combine the egg yolk, brandy, orange curaçao,
simple syrup, and half & half in a cocktail shaker
with ice. Shake vigorously for 10 seconds. Add
the champagne and stir. Strain into a cocktail
glass filled with crushed ice. Garnish with an
orange twist.

13

PYGMALIAN

Inspired by the classic My Fair Lady *champagne cocktail.*

2 STRAWBERRIES (1 FOR GARNISH)
½ OUNCE SIMPLE SYRUP (SEE PAGE 9)
1 SMALL EGG WHITE (OR 1 TABLESPOON
   PASTEURIZED EGG WHITE)
1 OUNCE ORANGE JUICE
1 OUNCE GIN
½ OUNCE CRÈME DE FRAISE LIQUEUR
   (STRAWBERRY LIQUEUR)
2 TO 3 OUNCES CHAMPAGNE

Muddle 1 strawberry with the simple syrup. (Use a muddler or the back of a spoon.) Add the egg white, orange juice, gin, and crème de fraise liqueur. Shake with ice. Add the champagne and stir. Strain into a glass filled with crushed ice. Garnish with a whole strawberry.

14

15
SPARKLING PISCO SOUR

1 SMALL EGG WHITE (OR 1 TABLESPOON
  PASTEURIZED EGG WHITE)
1 ½ OUNCES PISCO BRANDY
1 OUNCE SIMPLE SYRUP (SEE PAGE 9)
½ OUNCE FRESH LEMON JUICE
1 OUNCE CHAMPAGNE
ANGOSTURA BITTERS

Combine the egg white, brandy, simple syrup,
and lemon juice in a cocktail shaker with ice.
Shake vigorously for 10 seconds. Add the champagne and stir. Strain into a martini glass. Add a
dash of bitters on top and swirl with a toothpick.

FRAMBOISE CASSIS COCKTAIL

½ OUNCE CRÈME DE FRAMBOISE (OR
   RASPBERRY LIQUEUR)
½ OUNCE CRÈME DE CASSIS
1 RASPBERRY
1 BLACKBERRY
4 OUNCES CHAMPAGNE

Combine the crème de framboise, crème de cassis, raspberry, and blackberry in a cocktail shaker filled with ice, and shake vigorously. Add the champagne and stir. Strain into a champagne flute.

17
KIR ROYALE

5 OUNCES CHAMPAGNE
½ OUNCE CRÈME DE CASSIS (MARIE BRIZARD'S
   CASSIS DE BORDEAUX IS A GOOD CHOICE, IF
   IT IS AVAILABLE)
LEMON TWIST, FOR GARNISH

Fill a flute with chilled champagne. Add the crème de cassis and garnish with a lemon twist.

18
POM ROYALE

This is an easy-to-make and inexpensive sparkling cocktail that looks and tastes great. It can be served year-round. It is a variation of the classic Kir Royale.

3 TO 4 POMEGRANATE SEEDS OR DRIED
   CRANBERRIES, FOR GARNISH
¾ OUNCE POMEGRANATE LIQUEUR
5 OUNCES RED ROSSO SPUMANTE (AN
   INEXPENSIVE RED SPARKLING WINE FOUND
   IN MOST GROCERY OR LIQUOR STORES THAT
   IS A BIT SWEETER THAN CHAMPAGNE)
ORANGE TWIST, FOR GARNISH

Drop 3 to 4 pomegranate seeds (or dried cranberries) in the bottom of an empty champagne flute. Add the pomegranate liqueur. Top with the Red Rosso Spumante. Garnish with an orange twist and serve.

Pear Royale

Simple syrup (see page 9), for cocktail rim

2 tablespoons superfine sugar, for
  cocktail rim

½ ounce pear liqueur (Mathilde is a
  great choice)

½ ounce gin

4 ounces slightly sweet sparkling wine
  (e.g., Moët Nectar Imperial)

pear slice, for garnish

Wet the rim of a chilled champagne flute with simple syrup and dip into a plate of sugar several times to ensure coverage. Set aside. Combine the pear liqueur and gin in a cocktail shaker with ice and shake vigorously. Add the sparkling wine and stir. Strain into the sugar-rimmed champagne flute and garnish with a pear slice.

20
KIWI ROYALE

2 SLICES OF KIWI, CUT INTO QUARTERS, PLUS
  AN EXTRA SLICE FOR GARNISH (OPTIONAL)
1 OUNCE MIDORI
1 OUNCE PINEAPPLE JUICE
4 OUNCES SWEET SPARKLING WINE (E.G., MOËT
  NECTAR IMPERIAL)

Combine the kiwi, Midori, and pineapple juice in
a cocktail shaker with ice. Shake vigorously and
pour into a highball glass. Top off with sparkling
wine. Garnish with an additional kiwi slice, if
desired.

21
MIMOSA

This classic is probably the most popular champagne cocktail in the United States and most often served with breakfast or brunch. This is a great cocktail to have after New Year's Eve, to use all that leftover champagne. Feel free to substitute any citrus juice or nectar for the orange juice.

ORANGE JUICE (BEST IF FRESH SQUEEZED), OR
   ANY OTHER CITRUS JUICE
CHAMPAGNE

Fill a champagne flute about a third full of juice. Top off with champagne.

22
GRAND MIMOSA

Same recipe as above, but add $\frac{1}{2}$ ounce of Grand Marnier.

Miami Morning Mimosa

1 OUNCE RASPBERRY PUREE (SEE PAGE 8)
½ OUNCE COGNAC
½ OUNCE CRÈME DE BANANA LIQUEUR
3 TO 4 OUNCES SPARKLING WINE
SWEETENED WHIPPED CREAM, FOR GARNISH
(OPTIONAL)

Combine the raspberry puree, cognac, and crème de banana liqueur in a cocktail shaker with ice. Shake vigorously. Add the sparkling wine and stir. Strain into a chilled champagne flute. If desired, add a dollop of whipped cream for an à la mode version.

23

24
BUCK'S FIZZ

A classic cocktail from the 1920s. Same recipe as the Mimosa, just add a teaspoon of grenadine for color. It is also sometimes made with gin.

25
VALENCIA ROYALE

1 ½ OUNCES ORANGE JUICE
1 OUNCE APRICOT BRANDY
3 OUNCES CHAMPAGNE
ORANGE PEEL, FOR GARNISH

Combine the orange juice and apricot brandy in a cocktail shaker with ice. Shake vigorously and strain into a champagne flute. Top off with champagne and garnish with large piece of orange peel.

Tahitian Apricot Cocktail

1 ½ OUNCES APRICOT NECTAR
½ OUNCE NAVAN VANILLA LIQUEUR
½ OUNCE APRICOT BRANDY
3 OUNCES CHAMPAGNE
VANILLA BEAN, FOR GARNISH

Combine the apricot nectar, vanilla liqueur, and apricot brandy in a cocktail shaker with ice and shake moderately. Add the champagne and stir. Strain into a champagne flute and garnish with a vanilla bean.

26

Bellinis

Named after the famous the Italian painter Giovanni Bellini, this cocktail was created by Giovanni Cipriani at Harry's Bar in Venice, Italy, in the late 1940s. Originally it was made with the freshest of white peaches and an Italian sparkling wine, Prosecco. (The classic recipe is offered below.) But these days Bellinis are mixed from many different pureed fruits and juices, not just peach. So grab some fresh fruit and make your own Bellini!

27
CLASSIC BELLINI

If it is summertime and white peaches are in season, I highly recommend making your own white peach puree (see page 7). If you find that you like your Bellinis a little more peachy or the peaches are not quite ripe, feel free to add just a bit of a peach liqueur to make the flavor stand out a little more.

4 OUNCES PROSECCO SPARKLING WINE (OR CHAMPAGNE)
1 OUNCE WHITE PEACH PUREE

In a cocktail shaker combine the sparkling wine with the peach puree over ice. If desired, add a half ounce of peach liqueur for more punch. Stir until mixed and strain into a chilled champagne flute.

Guava Bellini

Same recipe as the Classic Bellini, just use an ounce of guava puree in lieu of the peach puree. If desired, add a half ounce of peach liqueur.

28

Berry Bellini

Same recipe as the Classic Bellini, just use an ounce of a berry puree (e.g., raspberry, blue-berry, strawberry, etc., see page 8) in lieu of the peach puree. If desired, add a half ounce of rasp-berry or peach liqueur.

29

30
JASMINE PEACH BELLINI

1 ½ OUNCES PEACH PUREE

½ OUNCE JASMINE SYRUP (OR 1 OUNCE
  SWEETENED JASMINE TEA)

SPLASH OF FRESH LEMON JUICE

3 TO 4 OUNCES CHAMPAGNE

Combine the peach puree, jasmine syrup, and lemon juice in a cocktail shaker with ice. Shake vigorously and strain into a chilled champagne flute. Top off with the champagne.

BLUEBERRY BELLINI

While a blueberry Bellini can simply be made with a blueberry puree, this variation gives it a little more complexity and flavor.

½ OUNCE PEACH LIQUEUR
½ OUNCE BLUEBERRY SYRUP (E.G., MONIN)
10 BLUEBERRIES
3 TO 4 OUNCES CHAMPAGNE

Muddle 7 blueberries with the peach liqueur and blueberry syrup in a cocktail shaker. (Use a muddler or the back of a spoon.) Add ice and shake vigorously. Add the champagne to the mixture and stir. Strain into a champagne flute and garnish with the 3 remaining blueberries.

31

32
APRICOT BELLINI

1 ½ OUNCES APRICOT NECTAR

¾ OUNCE COGNAC

¾ OUNCE APRICOT BRANDY

3 OUNCES CHAMPAGNE

MINT SPRIG, FOR GARNISH (OPTIONAL)

Combine the apricot nectar, cognac, and apricot brandy in a cocktail shaker with ice. Shake vigorously. Add the champagne and stir. Strain into a chilled champagne flute. Garnish with a mint sprig, if desired.

BELLINI TROPICALE

1 OUNCE MANGO PUREE
1 OUNCE PINEAPPLE JUICE
½ OUNCE PEACH LIQUEUR
4 OUNCES CHAMPAGNE

Combine the mango puree, pineapple juice, and peach liqueur in a cocktail shaker with ice. Shake vigorously. Add the champagne and stir. Strain into a chilled champagne flute. Garnish with a pineapple wedge or pineapple leaf.

33

BLOOD ORANGE BELLINI

1 OUNCE BLOOD ORANGE JUICE (OR PUREE)
1 teaspoon GRAND MARNIER
4 OUNCES CHAMPAGNE
ORANGE WHEEL, FOR GARNISH

Slice a thin orange wheel and place inside a champagne flute. Combine the blood orange juice and Grand Marnier in a cocktail shaker with ice. Shake vigorously and add the champagne. Stir, then strain into the champagne flute.

34

35
FROZEN BERRY BELLINI

½ CUP MIXED BERRIES (FRESH OR FROZEN),
  PLUS EXTRA FOR GARNISH
2 TO 3 OUNCES CHAMPAGNE
1 OUNCE SIMPLE SYRUP (SEE PAGE 9)
1 OUNCE PINEAPPLE JUICE

Combine all of the ingredients in a blender with
approximately 1 cup of ice. Blend until smooth.
Pour into small juice glasses and garnish with a
few berries.

Serves approximately 2

36
FROZEN BELLINI

½ CUP FROZEN OR FRESH PEACHES, PLUS A
  PEACH WEDGE FOR GARNISH (OPTIONAL)
3 OUNCES SWEET SPARKLING WINE (E.G.,
  CHANDON RICHE, OR MOSCATO D'ASTI)
1 OUNCE PEACH LIQUEUR
½ OUNCE SIMPLE SYRUP (SEE PAGE 9)

Combine all of the ingredients with approximately 1 cup of ice. Blend until smooth. Pour
into small juice glasses. Garnish with a peach
wedge, if desired.

Serves approximately 2

Sorbet Bellinis

Sorbet is a great ingredient to use with champagne; the tart fruitiness lends itself nicely to young sparkling wines. And with so many great sorbets and sparkling wines on the market, it's easy to make a good sorbet Bellini.

37
SILK WITH CHAMPAGNE (SOYER AU CHAMPAGNE)

Created in 1888, this is one of the first champagne cocktails that used ice cream. This recipe was taken from Ted Haigh's book, Vintage Spirits and Forgotten Cocktails *(Gloucester, Mass.: Quarry Books, 2004).*

- 2 DASHES MARASCHINO LIQUEUR
- 2 DASHES PINEAPPLE JUICE
- 2 DASHES ORANGE CURAÇAO (OR GRAND MARNIER)
- 2 DASHES BRANDY
- CHAMPAGNE
- 1 SPOONFUL VANILLA ICE CREAM

In a cocktail or parfait glass, combine the maraschino liqueur, pineapple juice, orange curaçao, and brandy. Top with champagne. Add the vanilla ice cream. Serve with a small spoon and straw.

APEACH SORBET BELLINI

3 SPOONFULS PEACH OR MANGO SORBET,
  SOFTENED
¾ OUNCE PEACH LIQUEUR
½ OUNCE ABSOLUT APEACH VODKA
SPLASH OF FRESH LEMON JUICE
CHAMPAGNE

Place the sorbet in the bottom of a champagne flute and set aside. Combine the peach liqueur, vodka, and lemon juice in a cocktail shaker with ice. Shake vigorously and strain into the champagne flute over the sorbet. Top off with champagne. Serve with a straw.

38

Lemon Rosé Bellini

1 SPOONFUL LEMON SORBET, SOFTENED
½ OUNCE CITRUS VODKA (OPTIONAL, FOR A STRONGER DRINK)
4 OUNCES ROSÉ CHAMPAGNE
2 TO 3 RASPBERRIES, FOR GARNISH

Combine the sorbet with the vodka in a cocktail shaker with ice. Shake vigorously. Add the champagne and stir. Strain into a chilled champagne flute and garnish with floating raspberries.

39

40
Mandarin Blossom Bellini

1 ½ OUNCES HANGAR 1 MANDARIN BLOSSOM
   VODKA
1 SPOONFUL OF PEACH SORBET (SOFT)
SPLASH OF FRESH LEMON JUICE
4 OUNCES CHAMPAGNE
ORANGE WHEEL, FOR GARNISH
MINT SPRIG, FOR GARNISH

Slice a thin orange wheel and place inside a champagne flute, against the side of the glass. Combine
the vodka, peach sorbet, and lemon juice in a
cocktail shaker with ice. Shake vigorously. Add the
champagne and stir. Strain into the champagne
flute. Garnish with a mint sprig.

LADY TEMPTATION

1 SPOONFUL LEMON SORBET, SOFTENED
½ OUNCE DAMIANA (A MEXICAN HERBAL
  LIQUEUR)
SPLASH OF REPOSADO TEQUILA
3 OUNCES CHAMPAGNE

Combine the lemon sorbet, Damiana, and tequila
in a cocktail shaker with ice. Shake vigorously.
Add the champagne and stir. Strain into a champagne flute.

41

42
HOPE FLOATS

*Created by master mixologist Bridget Albert from
Southern Wine & Spirits.*

1 ½ OUNCES **PAMA** POMEGRANATE LIQUEUR
2 OUNCES PINK GRAPEFRUIT JUICE
1 OUNCE CITRUS VODKA
SCOOP OF RASPBERRY SORBET
MARTINI & ROSSI ASTI SPUMANTE
MINT SPRIG, FOR GARNISH

Combine the pomegranate liqueur, grapefruit
juice, and citrus vodka in a cocktail shaker with
ice. Shake and strain into a cocktail glass. Add the
scoop of raspberry sorbet and top with Martini &
Rossi Asti Spumante. Garnish with a mint sprig.

43
ITALIAN MANGO BELLINI

1 SCOOP MANGO SORBET, SOFTENED
½ OUNCE CAMPARI
4 OUNCES PROSECCO

Combine the mango sorbet with the Campari in a cocktail shaker with ice. Shake vigorously. Add the Prosecco and stir. Strain into a champagne flute.

44
RASPBERRY SORBET BELLINI

1 SCOOP RASPBERRY SORBET, SOFTENED
½ OUNCE RASPBERRY LIQUEUR
½ OUNCE CITRUS VODKA (OPTIONAL)
CHAMPAGNE

Combine the raspberry sorbet, raspberry liqueur, and citrus vodka, if desired, in a cocktail shaker with ice. Shake vigorously. Add the champagne and stir. Strain into a champagne flute.

ADAM & EVE

This is a duo cocktail that can be served side-by-side.
It is a great romantic poolside drink.

4 SCOOPS LEMON OR PASSIONFRUIT SORBET,
   SOFTENED
3 OUNCES CITRUS VODKA
1 OUNCE POMEGRANATE JUICE
1 CUP SWEET SPARKLING WINE (E.G.,
   BALLATORE GRAN SPUMANTE)
LONG MINT SPRIGS, FOR GARNISH

Place 2 scoops of softened sorbet in each glass.
(A tall pilsner glass works beautifully.) Add $1\frac{1}{2}$
ounces of the citrus vodka to each glass. Add the
pomegranate juice to just one of the glasses. Top
off both glasses with a sweet sparkling wine and
garnish with a long mint sprig. Serve with a spoon
and straw.

Serves 2

45

BLUE CHAMPAGNE

CHAMPAGNE

1 OUNCE BLUE CURAÇAO

LEMON TWIST, FOR GARNISH

Fill a champagne flute with champagne about
$^3/_4$ full. Add the blue curaçao. Garnish with a
lemon twist.

46

47

SPARKLING ROSÉS

3 RED ROSE PETALS, RINSED WELL

1 OUNCE SIMPLE SYRUP (SEE PAGE 9)

4 OUNCES ROSÉ CHAMPAGNE (E.G., CHANDON
ROSÉ IMPERIAL)

In a cocktail shaker, muddle the rose petals with the simple syrup. (Use a muddler or the back of a spoon.) Add the ice and shake vigorously. Add the champagne and stir. Loosely strain into a champagne flute.

48

WHITE LAVENDER

¾ OUNCE GIN

¾ OUNCE PARFAIT AMOUR (A LAVENDER-
COLORED ORANGE LIQUEUR)

3 TO 4 OUNCES CHAMPAGNE

LAVENDER SPRIG, FOR GARNISH

Combine the gin and parfait amour in a cocktail shaker with ice. Shake vigorously and strain into a champagne flute. Top off with the chilled champagne. Garnish with a lavender sprig.

BELLINI TINI

**2 OUNCES PEACH NECTAR (OR 1½ OUNCES
PEACH PUREE)
1½ OUNCES PREMIUM CITRUS VODKA
1 OUNCE CRÈME DE PECHE LIQUEUR
SPLASH OF FRESH LEMON JUICE
CHAMPAGNE
LEMON WHEEL, FOR GARNISH**

Combine the peach nectar, citrus vodka, crème
de peche liqueur, and lemon juice in a cocktail
shaker with ice. Shake vigorously and strain into a
chilled martini glass. Top off with champagne.
Garnish with a floating lemon wheel.

49

Siren's Song

3 OUNCES CHAMPAGNE
1 OUNCE GINGER BEER
½ OUNCE RASPBERRY PUREE (SEE PAGE 8)
½ OUNCE RASPBERRY LIQUEUR

Combine all of the ingredients in a cocktail shaker with ice and stir for 5 to 10 seconds. Strain into a champagne flute.

50

Black Cherry Champagne

3 PITTED BLACK CHERRIES
1 OUNCE CHERRY HEERING BRANDY
½ OUNCE FRESH LEMON JUICE
½ OUNCE SIMPLE SYRUP (SEE PAGE 9)
CHAMPAGNE

In a cocktail shaker, muddle the pitted cherries with the Cherry Heering, lemon juice, and simple syrup. (Use a muddler or the back of a spoon.) Add ice and shake vigorously. Pour into a highball glass and add more ice, if desired. Top off with champagne. Garnish with an additional black cherry, if desired.

To serve this cocktail in a champagne flute, simply strain the contents after shaking and top off with champagne.

51

52

BELLINI HIGHBALL

3 TO 4 SLICED PEACHES, PLUS AN EXTRA WEDGE
FOR GARNISH (OPTIONAL)
1 OUNCE PEACH PUREE
½ OUNCE PEACH SCHNAPPS
3 TO 4 OUNCES CHAMPAGNE

Combine the peaches, peach puree, and peach
schnapps in a cocktail shaker with ice. Shake moderately. Pour into a highball glass and top off with
champagne. Stir and serve. Garnish with an additional peach wedge, if desired.

53

BERRY BELLINI HIGHBALL

2 SLICED PEACHES
HANDFUL OF FRESH BERRIES (E.G., BLUE-
BERRIES, RASPBERRIES, BLACKBERRIES,
SLICED STRAWBERRIES)
1 OUNCE PEACH PUREE
½ OUNCE PEACH SCHNAPPS
3 TO 4 OUNCES CHAMPAGNE (ROSÉ IS BEST)

Combine the peaches, berries, peach puree, and
peach schnapps in a cocktail shaker with ice. Shake
moderately. Pour into a highball glass and top off
with champagne. Stir and serve.

BADA BING

2 BASIL LEAVES, SLICED INTO THIN STRIPS
3 PITTED BING CHERRIES, PLUS 2 EXTRA FOR
 GARNISH (OPTIONAL)
1 OUNCE PLYMOUTH GIN
½ OUNCE SIMPLE SYRUP (SEE PAGE 9)
½ OUNCE MARASCHINO LIQUEUR
½ OUNCE FRESH LIME JUICE
3 TO 4 OUNCES CHAMPAGNE

Combine the basil, cherries, gin, simple syrup,
maraschino liqueur, and lime juice in a cocktail
shaker with crushed ice. Shake moderately and
pour into a highball glass. (Add more crushed ice,
if needed.) Top off with the champagne and stir.
If desired, garnish with 2 additional skewered
Bing cherries.

54

55

KUMQUAT PÊCHE HIGHBALL

1 RIPE KUMQUAT, SLICED

2 PEACH SLICES

5 MINT LEAVES, PLUS AN ADDITIONAL MINT
SPRIG FOR GARNISH (OPTIONAL)

1 OUNCE CRÈME DE PÊCHE LIQUEUR (SIMILAR
TO PEACH SCHNAPPS)

1 OUNCE ORANGE JUICE

3 OUNCES CHAMPAGNE (LIGHT AND SEMISWEET;
DEMI-SEC OR MOSCATO D'ASTI WOULD BE A
GOOD CHOICE)

Combine the kumquat, peach slices, mint, crème de pêche liqueur, and orange juice in a cocktail shaker with ice. Shake vigorously and pour into a highball glass. Add more ice and top off with champagne. Stir and garnish with an additional mint sprig, if desired.

APHRODISIA

This cocktail is the ultimate in berry decadence and sure to please. The more berries, the merrier.

½ CUP BLUEBERRIES, OR ANY COMBINATION OF
   SEASONAL BERRIES (E.G., BLACKBERRIES,
   RASPBERRIES, BOYSENBERRIES)
2 STRAWBERRIES, HULLED AND SLICED
1 OUNCE NAVAN VANILLA LIQUEUR
¾ OUNCE SIMPLE SYRUP (SEE PAGE 9)
2 TO 3 OUNCES RED ROSSO SPUMANTE (OR A
   SEMISWEET ROSÉ SPARKLING WINE)

Muddle the berries with the Navan vanilla liqueur and simple syrup. (Use a muddler or the back of a spoon.) Add ice and shake vigorously. Pour into a highball or tall pilsner glass. (Add more ice, if needed.) Top off with the spumante and stir. Add additional fruit on the top—pile it on! Serve with a straw. You may also want to include a small cocktail pick to pluck off all the berries.

56

57
BRUNCH MARGARITA

Taken from my first book in the 101 series, 101
Margaritas, *(John Wiley & Sons, 2006).*

¾ OUNCE ORANGE JUICE

¾ OUNCE PINK LEMONADE

¾ OUNCE PINEAPPLE JUICE

½ OUNCE TEQUILA

½ OUNCE TRIPLE SEC

2 OUNCES CHAMPAGNE (OR SPARKLING WINE)

ORANGE, PINEAPPLE, OR LEMON SLICE OR
   WEDGE, FOR GARNISH

Combine the orange juice, pink lemonade,
pineapple juice, tequila, and triple sec in a cocktail shaker filled with ice and shake vigorously.
Pour into a margarita glass. Top off with champagne. Garnish with a fruit slice or wedge.

SPARKLING CANTALOUPE CUP

4 CANTALOUPE BALLS
1 LEMON WHEEL, CUT INTO QUARTERS
1 LIME WHEEL, CUT INTO QUARTERS
1 OUNCE VODKA
3 TO 4 OUNCES CHAMPAGNE

Combine the cantaloupe, lemon, lime, and vodka in a cocktail shaker filled with ice. Shake vigorously and pour into a highball glass. Add additional ice and top off with champagne. Stir and serve.

58

The next three cocktails are all infusions topped off with champagne. I created these for an event at the Food & Wine Classic (Aspen, Colorado), which is held just a few weeks before July 4th. People loved them, and they were perfect in the hot afternoon sun. As the afternoon progressed, we just referred to the cocktails as Red, White, and Blue.

Note: The infusions themselves are very fruit forward and on the sweet side; they are specifically made to be mixed with champagne. The champagne adds a nice acidic and fizzy counterbalance to the sweet, fruity base.

59
SPARKLING RASPBERRY COCKTAIL (AKA "RED")

2 OUNCES RED RASPBERRY INFUSION
  (SEE OPPOSITE)
3 TO 4 OUNCES CHANDON ROSÉ IMPERIAL
  CHAMPAGNE
1 TO 2 RASPBERRIES, FOR GARNISH

Fill a highball glass or tall flute glass with ice. Add 2 ounces of the Red Raspberry Infusion. Top off with the Chandon Rosé Imperial champagne. Stir with a straw and garnish with a raspberry or two.

Red Raspberry Infusion

1 LITER BELVEDERE VODKA, OR OTHER
  PREMIUM VODKA
½ LITER GRAND MARNIER
3 PINTS RASPBERRIES
2 PINTS STRAWBERRIES, HULLED AND SLICED
1 BUNCH OF MINT, CLEANED AND PLUCKED
1 ½ CUPS SIMPLE SYRUP (SEE PAGE 9)
¾ CUP FRESH LIME JUICE

In a large glass infusion jar (with a spigot), combine all of the ingredients. Cover and keep refrigerated for 24 to 48 hours. Prior to serving, scoop
out the majority of the fruit to use as a garnish.
(This also prevents bits of fruit from getting
caught in the spigot.)

60

Sparkling Lychee–Pear Cocktail (aka "White")

2 OUNCES WHITE PEAR–LYCHEE INFUSION
   (SEE RECIPE BELOW)
3 TO 4 OUNCES CHANDON NECTAR CHAMPAGNE
   (A SEMISWEET CHAMPAGNE)
PEAR SLICE, FOR GARNISH

Fill a highball glass or tall flute glass with ice. Add 2 ounces of the White Pear–Lychee Infusion. Top off with the Chandon Nectar champagne. Stir and garnish with a pear slice.

White Pear–Lychee Infusion

1 LITER CHOPIN VODKA, OR OTHER PREMIUM
   VODKA
2 15-OUNCE CANS WHOLE LYCHEE FRUIT
   (WITH THE SYRUP)
3 BARTLETT PEARS, CORED AND SLICED
1½ CUPS FRESH LEMON JUICE

In a large glass infusion jar (with a spigot), combine all of the ingredients. Cover and keep refrigerated for 24 to 48 hours. Prior to serving, scoop out the majority of the fruit to use as a garnish. (This also prevents bits of fruit from getting caught in the spigot.)

61

BLACK & BLUE CHAMPAGNE COCKTAIL (AKA "BLUE")

2 OUNCES BLACK & BLUE BERRY INFUSION
   (SEE BELOW)
4 OUNCES CHANDON WHITE STAR CHAMPAGNE
3 TO 4 BLUEBERRIES, FOR GARNISH

Fill a highball glass or tall flute glass with ice.
Add the Black & Blue Infusion. Top off with the
Chandon White Star champagne. Stir with a straw
and garnish with additional blueberries.

BLACK & BLUE BERRY INFUSION

1 LITER BELVEDERE VODKA, OR OTHER
   PREMIUM VODKA
½ LITER MONIN BLUEBERRY SYRUP
2 PINTS BLUEBERRIES
2 PINTS BLACKBERRIES
1 BUNCH OF MINT
1 ½ CUPS FRESH LIME JUICE

In a large glass infusion jar (with a spigot), combine all of the ingredients. Cover and keep
refrigerated for 24 to 48 hours. Prior to serving,
scoop out the majority of the fruit to use as a garnish. (This also prevents bits of fruit from getting caught in the spigot.)

SPARKLING POIRE

PEAR SLICE, FOR GARNISH

½ CUP DICED BARTLETT PEAR (OR 1 OUNCE
    MATHILDE PEAR LIQUEUR)

½ OUNCE SIMPLE SYRUP (SEE PAGE 9)

4 OUNCES CHANDON BRUT CHAMPAGNE

Cut a whole pear into slices, lengthwise (approximately ⅛ inch thick.) Slice in half again, lengthwise. Place a slice of pear in a champagne flute and set aside.

In a cocktail shaker, muddle the diced pear with the simple syrup. (Use a muddler or the back of a spoon.) Add ice and shake vigorously. Add the champagne to the mix and stir. Strain into the champagne flute over the pear slice.

CHAMPAGNE COOLER

This cocktail was created for the Riunite wine group. A delicious cocktail that is light and fruity . . . and a little retro-hip. Feel free to add any fruit you like—whatever you find in your fridge or at your local grocery store— for a fresh perspective.

ORANGE WHEEL, FOR GARNISH

1 ½ OUNCES FRESH SOUR (SEE PAGE 9)

½ OUNCE TRIPLE SEC

HANDFUL OF FRESH FRUIT, IF DESIRED
(ANYTHING FROM DICED ORANGES TO BERRIES
TO DICED MELON)

3 OUNCES RIUNITE D'ORO (A SPARKLING RED
WINE, AVAILABLE ALMOST ANYWHERE IN THE
UNITED STATES)

Place an entire orange wheel in a champagne flute. Press the orange wheel against the champagne flute wall. (If the orange is oversized, cut the wheel in half.)

In a cocktail shaker, combine the fresh sour and triple sec with ice. If desired, add a handful or so of diced fruit or berries. Shake vigorously and strain into the garnished champagne flute. Top off with Riunite D'Oro.

64
SPARKLING APPLE COCKTAIL

1 OUNCE APPLE JUICE
½ OUNCE COGNAC
½ OUNCE SIMPLE SYRUP (SEE PAGE 9)
4 TO 5 RED OR GREEN APPLE CHUNKS
3 OUNCES CHAMPAGNE

Combine the apple juice, cognac, simple syrup, and apple chunks in a cocktail shaker with ice. Shake vigorously and pour into a cocktail glass. Add additional ice, if needed. Top off with champagne. Stir and serve.

65
SPARKLING MOJITO

7 TO 10 MINT LEAVES, PLUS A SPRIG FOR GARNISH
1 OUNCE SIMPLE SYRUP (SEE PAGE 9)
JUICE OF 1 LIME (ABOUT 1 OUNCE)
¾ OUNCE CITRUS VODKA
¾ OUNCE LIGHT RUM
1½ OUNCES CHANDON BRUT CLASSIC CHAMPAGNE

In a cocktail shaker, muddle the mint leaves with the simple syrup and lime juice. (Use a muddler or the back of a spoon.) Add the citrus vodka and rum. Add crushed ice. Top with Chandon Brut Classic and stir. Garnish with a mint sprig.

66
SPARKLING MARGARITA

Taken from my first book in the 101 series, 101
Margaritas *(John Wiley & Sons, 2006).*

1 OUNCE TEQUILA
1 OUNCE FRESH LEMON JUICE
1 OUNCE SIMPLE SYRUP (SEE PAGE 9)
½ OUNCE COINTREAU
2 OUNCES CHAMPAGNE (OR SPARKLING WINE)
LEMON TWIST, FOR GARNISH

Combine the tequila, lemon juice, simple syrup,
and Cointreau in a martini shaker and shake vigorously. Strain into a champagne flute. Top off with
champagne. Garnish with a lemon twist. This cocktail can also be served in a cocktail glass with ice.

SPARKLING STRAWBERRY MARGARITA

1 OUNCE REPOSADO TEQUILA

1 OUNCE FRESH SOUR (SEE PAGE 9)

½ OUNCE CRÈME DE CASSIS

½ OUNCE SIMPLE SYRUP (SEE PAGE 9)

3 STRAWBERRIES, PLUS 1 FOR GARNISH

5 MINT LEAVES

2 OUNCES CHAMPAGNE

Combine the tequila, fresh sour, crème de cassis, simple syrup, strawberries, and mint leaves in a cocktail shaker with ice. Shake vigorously. Add the champagne, stir, and pour into a tall pilsner glass. Add more ice, if needed. Garnish with a strawberry.

67

Pink Pussycat

3 STRAWBERRIES (1 FOR GARNISH)
1 OUNCE COCONUT CREAM (E.G., COCO LOPEZ)
1 OUNCE CRÈME DE BANANA LIQUEUR
½ OUNCE COGNAC
3 TO 4 OUNCES CHAMPAGNE

Hull and slice 2 of the strawberries and drop into a cocktail shaker. Add the coconut cream, crème de banana liqueur, cognac, and ice. Shake vigorously. Add the champagne to the mix and stir. Strain into a cocktail glass filled with ice. Garnish with a whole strawberry.

68

69

WATERMELON FRIZZY

½ CUP FRESH WATERMELON (SEEDLESS)
1 ORANGE WHEEL, CUT INTO QUARTERS
5 MINT LEAVES, PLUS A SPRIG FOR GARNISH
1 OUNCE PREMIUM VODKA
½ OUNCE SIMPLE SYRUP (SEE PAGE 9)
1 ½ TO 2 OUNCES CHANDON ROSÉ CHAMPAGNE

In a cocktail shaker, muddle the watermelon,
orange, and mint leaves with the vodka and simple
syrup. (Use a muddler or the back of a spoon.)
Add a small amount of ice and shake vigorously.
Pour into a stem or highball glass. Add additional
crushed ice and top off with Chandon Rosé.
Garnish with a mint sprig.

70
Huckleberry Thyme Fizz

From the kitchen of Kathy Casey Food Studios.
Huckleberries are similar to blueberries and are in sea-
son in the fall. If you are unable to find them, feel free
to use blueberries or any other seasonal berry.

1 FRESH THYME SPRIG, PLUS 1 FOR GARNISH
¾ OUNCE HUCKLEBERRY-INFUSED VODKA
   (SEE RECIPE BELOW)
¾ OUNCE HIGH QUALITY VODKA
¾ OUNCE FRESH LEMON JUICE
¾ OUNCE SIMPLE SYRUP (SEE PAGE 9)
SPLASH OF CHAMPAGNE
TWISTED LEMON ZEST

Bend 1 thyme sprig to release the flavor and drop
into a cocktail shaker. Add the vodkas, lemon
juice, and simple syrup. Fill with ice, cap, and
shake vigorously. Strain into a large martini glass
and top with champagne. Garnish with a fresh
thyme sprig and lemon zest.

HUCKLEBERRY–INFUSED VODKA

Infuse 3 cups of vodka with 2 cups of fresh huckleberries (crushed) for 2 to 3 days and strain. If
fresh huckleberries are not available, you can substitute any other local berry.

Sparkling Fruit Bath

This is a great summertime sparkling "fruit salad"—an eruption of fresh fruits bathed in champagne! Perfect for the outdoors and for large groups of people.

1 WHOLE WATERMELON
6 CUPS SEASONAL FRUIT, CUT INTO BITE-SIZED
    PIECES (E.G., PINEAPPLE, CANTALOUPE,
    GRAPES, BERRIES)
1 BOTTLE SPARKLING WINE (BALLATORE GRAN
    SPUMANTE IS A GREAT CHOICE)

MARINATING RECIPE:
4 CUPS CITRUS OR OTHER FLAVORED VODKA
2 CUPS GRAND MARNIER
2 CUPS SIMPLE SYRUP (SEE PAGE 9)

Cut a watermelon in half. Scoop out watermelon flesh using a melon baller; discard all seeds. Scrape the insides, making a clean bowl; set aside.

Prepare the marinating recipe by combining the vodka, Grand Marnier, and simple syrup in a pitcher and set aside. In a very large bowl (you may want to use a punch bowl), combine the watermelon balls and any seasonal fruit. Add the marinating mixture to the fruit, and let sit covered and refrigerated for at least 2 hours (best if overnight).

When ready to use, drain the fruit and place in the empty watermelon bowl. Immediately prior to serving, top off with sparkling wine and serve with forks.

71

SPRINGTIME SPARKLER

2 SCOOPS LEMON SORBET, SOFTENED

1 TO 2 OUNCES HENDRICKS GIN (WHILE YOU
   MAY USE ANOTHER GIN, HENDRICKS HAS
   SOME ROSE NOTES THAT ACCENT THIS
   COCKTAIL NICELY)

½ OUNCE ST. GERMAINE ELDERFLOWER
   LIQUEUR (OPTIONAL)

CHAMPAGNE

3 TO 4 EDIBLE FLOWERS (CAN SOMETIMES BE
   FOUND IN THE PRODUCE SECTION OF
   GROCERY STORES)

Scoop the lemon sorbet into a tall cocktail glass. Add the gin and elderflower cordial (if desired). Top with champagne and stir. Top with edible flowers, and serve with a spoon and straw.

72

73
SPARKLING MOJITO ICE

This is a sparkling mojito served granita style. Perfect for those hot summer months. It looks great served in the two-piece martini glasses where martini "top" fits inside a bowl of crushed ice.

2 CUPS FRESH SOUR (SEE PAGE 9)
20 MINT LEAVES
CHAMPAGNE (SWEET, E.G., BALLATORE GRAN SPUMANTE)

Before starting, make sure there is enough room in your freezer to easily fit a 9 × 13 pan. Pour the fresh sour into the pan. Place the mint leaves on top of the mixture and spread leaves out evenly, making sure they are not all clumped together. Place the pan in the freezer and let freeze (approximately 4 to 6 hours.) Place the sparkling wine in the refrigerator to keep chilled.

Once the mixture is frozen and you are ready to serve, use a spoon to scrape the icy mixture into a fine ice. Spoon into martini glasses, making a mound of ice. Slowly pour in the sparkling wine, 1 to 2 ounces per glass, and serve.

Caipirinha Caramba

A caipirinha is a classic Brazilian cocktail made from cachaça (a strong Brazilian rum) and fresh muddled lime. This is a variation made with cherries and champagne!

3 PITTED BLACK CHERRIES

2 LIME QUARTERS

1 OUNCE SIMPLE SYRUP (SEE PAGE 9)

1 OUNCE CACHAÇA

3 OUNCES CHAMPAGNE

Combine the pitted cherries, lime quarters, and simple syrup in a cocktail shaker. Muddle the fruit until the juice has been extracted from the lime quarters and the cherries are pulped. (Use a muddler or the back of a spoon.) Add the cachaça and ice. Shake vigorously and pour into a cocktail glass. Add more ice, if desired, and top off with the champagne.

74

Starfish Cooler

*This cocktail was an award winner at the 2007
Champagne Cocktail Competition at Tales of the
Cocktail, New Orleans, an annual event dedicated to
preserving the craft of the cocktail. This cooler was
created by Stacey Smith.*

2 ORANGE QUARTERS
3 TO 4 MINT LEAVES, PLUS A SPRIG FOR GARNISH
½ OUNCE SIMPLE SYRUP (SEE PAGE 9)
1 OUNCE LIMONCELLO
1 OUNCE PAMA POMEGRANATE LIQUEUR
1 OUNCE UNSWEETENED ICED TEA
MOËT WHITE STAR SPARKLING WINE

In a cocktail shaker, muddle the orange quarters,
mint leaves, and simple syrup. (Use a muddler or
the back of a spoon.) Add the limoncello, pomegranate liqueur, unsweetened iced tea, and ice.
Shake vigorously, and strain into a tall glass filled
with ice. Top off with Moët White Star sparkling
wine. Garnish with an additional mint sprig.

75

76
STORMY
GINGER FIZZ

This is a variation of the classic "Dark & Stormy" cocktail, with the light and bubbly kiss of champagne. A great cocktail to serve onboard ships or boats, as ginger helps to combat seasickness.

2 TO 3 PIECES FRESH SHAVED GINGER (OR
   ½ OUNCE GINGER JUICE)
4 LIME QUARTERS
5 TO 7 MINT LEAVES
1 OUNCE SIMPLE SYRUP (SEE PAGE 9)
1 ½ OUNCES LIGHT RUM
CHAMPAGNE (BRUT)

In a cocktail glass, muddle the fresh ginger with the lime quarters, mint leaves, and simple syrup. (Use a muddler or the back of a spoon.) Add the rum and ice and shake vigorously. Pour into a highball glass and top off with a brut champagne. Serve with a straw.

77

Champagne Julep

5 TO 7 MINT LEAVES, PLUS LONG MINT SPRIGS
   FOR GARNISH
½ OUNCE SIMPLE SYRUP (SEE PAGE 9)
1 ½ TO 2 OUNCES BOURBON
CHAMPAGNE (DRY)

In a cocktail glass, muddle the mint leaves with the simple syrup. (Use a muddler or the back of a spoon.) Add the bourbon and fill with crushed ice. Top off with champagne and stir. Garnish with mint sprigs.

78

Champagne Old-Fashioned

2 ORANGE QUARTERS
1 CHERRY, PLUS 1 FOR GARNISH
½ OUNCE SIMPLE SYRUP (SEE PAGE 9)
½ OUNCE GRAND MARNIER
DASH OF BITTERS (CAN USE ANGOSTURA, BUT
   BETTER IF YOU CAN FIND ORANGE BITTERS)
LARGE PIECE OF ORANGE PEEL, FOR GARNISH
CHAMPAGNE (BRUT)

In a cocktail shaker, muddle the orange quarters and a cherry with the simple syrup, Grand Marnier, and bitters. (Use a muddler or the back of a spoon.) Add ice and shake moderately. Strain into an empty cocktail glass. Fill with ice, top with champagne, and stir. Garnish with an additional cherry and a large piece of orange peel.

NEW WILLIAM COCKTAIL

1 ½ OUNCES PEAR NECTAR

¾ OUNCE PEAR LIQUEUR

½ OUNCE MARASCHINO LIQUEUR

½ OUNCE FRESH LEMON JUICE

3 TO 4 THIN PEAR SLICES (BARTLETT PREFERRED)

3 OUNCES CHAMPAGNE

MARASCHINO CHERRY, FOR GARNISH

Combine the pear nectar, pear liqueur, maraschino liqueur, lemon juice, and pear slices in a cocktail shaker with ice. Shake vigorously, and pour into a cocktail glass. Top off with champagne and serve. Garnish with a maraschino cherry.

79

Happy Hemingway

A variation of the classic "Hemingway Daiquiri," made with champagne. Light, refreshing, and not too sweet.

2 OUNCES FRESH-SQUEEZED GRAPEFRUIT JUICE
1 OUNCE LIGHT RUM
½ OUNCE MARASCHINO LIQUEUR
½ OUNCES SIMPLE SYRUP (SEE PAGE 9)
DASH OF ANGOSTURA BITTERS
1 ½ OUNCES CHAMPAGNE
LEMON OR GRAPEFRUIT TWIST, FOR GARNISH

Combine the grapefruit juice, rum, maraschino liqueur, simple syrup, and bitters in a cocktail shaker with ice. Shake vigorously and strain into a chilled martini glass. Top off with the champagne. Garnish with a lemon or grapefruit twist.

80

81
MAGNOLIA

4 TO 5 MINT LEAVES

1 OUNCE FRESH LIME JUICE

1 OUNCE SIMPLE SYRUP (SEE PAGE 9)

¾ OUNCE GIN

½ OUNCE ELDERFLOWER LIQUEUR

CHAMPAGNE

WHITE ORCHID, FOR GARNISH

In a cocktail shaker, muddle the mint leaves with the simple syrup. (Use a muddler or the back of the spoon.) Add the lime juice, gin, and elderflower liqueur with ice. Shake vigorously, and pour into a highball glass. Add more ice, if necessary. Top off with champagne. Garnish with a white orchid.

BUBBLING RUBIES

2 OUNCES WHITE CRANBERRY JUICE
1 ½ OUNCES PREMIUM VODKA
¾ OUNCE PEACH LIQUEUR
SPLASH OF FRESH LIME JUICE
1 ½ OUNCES CHAMPAGNE
POMEGRANATE SEEDS, FOR GARNISH

Place a spoonful of pomegranate seeds in a chilled martini glass. In a cocktail shaker, combine the white cranberry juice, vodka, peach liqueur, and lime juice with ice. Shake vigorously, and strain into the chilled martini glass. Top with champagne and serve.

82

BUBBLING ROSÉ RUBIES

Same recipe as above, but substitute crème de cassis for the peach liqueur for this version.

83

84

PACIFIC STAR MARTINI

I created this cocktail for the Four Seasons Resort Maui—a light, tropical, sparkling martini.

2 OUNCES WHITE CRANBERRY JUICE
1 ½ OUNCES BELVEDERE VODKA
¾ OUNCE ORANGE CURAÇAO (OR TRIPLE SEC)
½ OUNCE MONIN LYCHEE SYRUP
½ OUNCE FRESH LEMON JUICE
CHAMPAGNE
STARFRUIT SLICE, FOR GARNISH

In a cocktail shaker, combine the cranberry juice, vodka, orange curaçao, lychee syrup, and lemon juice. Shake vigorously, and strain into a chilled martini glass. Top off with a splash of champagne. Garnish with a slice of starfruit.

85

SPARKLING MOJITO MARTINI

5 TO 7 MINT LEAVES

1 OUNCE FRESH LIME JUICE

1 OUNCE SIMPLE SYRUP (SEE PAGE 9)

1 ½ OUNCES CITRUS VODKA

1 ½ OUNCES LIGHT AND DRY CHAMPAGNE (E.G.,
   MOËT WHITE STAR)

Combine the mint leaves with the lime juice and
simple syrup. Muddle lightly and add the citrus
vodka and ice. (Use a muddler or the back of a
spoon.) Shake vigorously, and strain into a chilled
martini glass. Top off with champagne. Garnish
with an additional mint sprig.

86

GRAND FRAISE MARTINI

2 STRAWBERRIES, HULLED AND SLICED

1 BASIL LEAF, PLUS 1 FOR GARNISH

1 OUNCE SIMPLE SYRUP (SEE PAGE 9)

½ OUNCE GRAND MARNIER

3 TO 4 OUNCES ROSÉ CHAMPAGNE

In a mixing glass, muddle the strawberries with 1
basil leaf and the simple syrup. (Use a muddler or
the back of a spoon.) Add the Grand Marnier and
ice. Shake vigorously. Add the rosé champagne
and stir. Strain into a chilled martini glass.
Garnish with a floating basil leaf.

PINEAPPLE CHAMPAGNE MARTINI

This is taken from my second book in the 101 series,
101 Martinis *(John Wiley & Sons, 2006).*

3 OUNCES PINEAPPLE JUICE (FRESH OR BRAND
   NAME), OR SIX 1-INCH PIECES OF PINEAPPLE
1 OUNCE VODKA
3 OUNCES CHAMPAGNE
PINEAPPLE WEDGE, FOR GARNISH

Combine the pineapple juice and vodka (or muddle fresh pineapple pieces with a muddler or the
back of a spoon) in a cocktail shaker filled with ice.
Shake vigorously. Add the champagne to the shaker
and stir. Strain into a chilled martini glass.
Garnish with a pineapple wedge.

87

VERY SEXY MARTINI

Inspired by Tony Abou-Ganim's "Very Sexy Cocktail,"
this version includes a rosé champagne and is served
straight up. Très sexy!

3 TO 4 RASPBERRIES, PLUS 1 FOR GARNISH
5 TO 7 MINT LEAVES, PLUS A SPRIG FOR GARNISH
1 OUNCE FRESH LIME JUICE
1 OUNCE SIMPLE SYRUP (SEE PAGE 9)
1 ½ OUNCES PREMIUM CITRUS VODKA
1 ½ OUNCES ROSÉ CHAMPAGNE (E.G., MOËT
   ROSÉ IMPERIAL CHAMPAGNE)

Combine the raspberries, mint, lime juice, and
simple syrup in a cocktail shaker and muddle. (Use
a muddler or the back of a spoon.) Add the citrus
vodka and ice. Shake vigorously and double-strain
into a chilled martini glass. Top off with Moët
Rosé Imperial champagne. Garnish with an additional mint sprig and a raspberry.

88

89
LIMONCELLO SPARKLE

1 OUNCE LIMONCELLO (AN ITALIAN LEMON
   LIQUEUR)
½ OUNCE COINTREAU
CHAMPAGNE
LONG LEMON PEEL, FOR GARNISH

Combine the limoncello and Cointreau in a
cocktail shaker with ice. Shake moderately, and
strain into a champagne flute. Top with champagne. Garnish with a long lemon peel.

90
ROSY LIMONCELLO SPARKLE

Same recipe as above, but add 4 to 5 raspberries
to the mixture and top with a rosé champagne.

GOLDEN BANANA

½ OUNCE LIGHT RUM
½ OUNCE CRÈME DE BANANA
GOLD FLAKES, FOR GARNISH
CHAMPAGNE

Combine the rum and crème de banana in a cocktail shaker with ice. Shake vigorously and strain into a champagne flute. Add gold flakes. Top off with champagne and serve.

91

TROPICAL ROMANCE

3 TO 4 PINEAPPLE CHUNKS (APPROXIMATELY
  1 INCH × 1 INCH)
1 ½ OUNCES COCONUT RUM
½ OUNCE SIMPLE SYRUP (SEE PAGE 9)
3 OUNCES SWEET SPARKLING WINE (E.G.,
  BALLATORE GRAN SPUMANTE)
PINEAPPLE WEDGE OR LONG PINEAPPLE LEAF,
  FOR GARNISH

In a cocktail shaker, muddle the pineapple chunks with the coconut rum and simple syrup. (Use a muddler or the back of a spoon.) Add ice and shake vigorously. Strain into a champagne flute and top off with the sparkling wine. Garnish with either a pineapple wedge or long pineapple leaf.

92

93
SPARKLING MANGO MARTINI

This is taken from my second book in the 101 series,
101 Martinis *(John Wiley & Sons, 2006).*

3 OUNCES MANGO PUREE (SEE PAGE 9)
2 OUNCES VODKA
SPLASH OF FRESH LEMON JUICE
3 OUNCES CHAMPAGNE
BASIL LEAF, FOR GARNISH

Combine the mango puree, vodka, and lemon juice
in a cocktail shaker, and shake vigorously. Add the
champagne to the shaker and stir. Strain into a
chilled martini glass. Garnish with a basil leaf.

94
SPARKLING PEAR MARTINI

PEAR SLICE, FOR GARNISH
2 OUNCES FRESH SOUR (SEE PAGE 9)
1 ½ OUNCES PREMIUM CITRUS VODKA
¾ OUNCE PEAR LIQUEUR
1 OUNCE CHAMPAGNE

Slice a whole pear lengthwise, approximately ½
inch thick. Place a slice in a chilled martini glass,
and set aside. Combine the fresh sour, vodka, and
pear liqueur in a cocktail shaker filled with ice,
and shake vigorously. Strain into the chilled martini glass over the pear slice and top off with
champagne.

DONA DE LA NOCHE

This was created by Francesco LaFranconi, the director of mixology and spirits educator for Southern Wine & Spirits of America.

SIMPLE SYRUP (SEE PAGE 9), FOR MARTINI RIM
CINNAMON-SUGAR MIX, FOR MARTINI RIM
1 OUNCE PINEAPPLE JUICE
1 OUNCE COCONUT PUREE (OR SWEETENED
   COCONUT CREAM, E.G., COCO LOPEZ)
1 OUNCE PYRAT XO RUM
½ OUNCE DISARONNO ORIGINALE AMARETTO
2 OUNCES EXTRA-DRY CHAMPAGNE

Wet the rim of a martini glass in simple syrup. Dip into the cinnamon-sugar mix several times to ensure coverage, and set aside. In a cocktail shaker, combine the pineapple juice, coconut puree, rum, and amaretto with ice. Shake vigorously. Add the champagne and stir. Strain into the cinnamon-sugar rimmed martini glass.

95

96
POINSETTIA
COCKTAIL

A simple, elegant cocktail. Great and easy to make for the holidays.

½ OUNCE ORANGE LIQUEUR (E.G., GRAND
    MARNIER, COINTREAU, TRIPLE SEC)
3 OUNCES CRANBERRY JUICE, CHILLED
ORANGE TWIST (IT LOOKS GREAT IF YOU HAVE A
    CHANNEL KNIFE AND CAN CUT A LONG
    ORANGE SPIRAL)
CHAMPAGNE, CHILLED

In a champagne flute, combine the orange liqueur and the chilled cranberry juice. Add the orange twist, top with champagne, and serve. This can also be served in a wine glass.

DOUGLAS FIR SPARKLETINI

Created by Kathy Casey of Kathy Casey Food Studios, 2006.

1 ½ OUNCES DOUGLAS FIR–INFUSED GIN (SEE
   RECIPE BELOW)
¾ OUNCE FRESH LEMON JUICE
¾ OUNCE SIMPLE SYRUP (SEE PAGE 9)
¾ OUNCE WHITE CRANBERRY JUICE
1 TO 1 ½ OUNCES BRUT CHAMPAGNE OR DRY
   SPARKLING WINE
TINY DOUGLAS FIR SPRIG AND A FROZEN
   CRANBERRY, FOR GARNISH

Fill a cocktail shaker with ice. Add the infused gin, lemon juice, simple syrup, and white cranberry juice. Shake vigorously and strain into a large martini glass. Top off with champagne. Garnish with a Douglas fir sprig and a whole frozen cranberry.

DOUGLAS FIR–INFUSED GIN
1 BOTTLE PREMIUM GIN
5- TO 6-INCH DOUGLAS FIR BRANCH, RINSED

Place Douglas fir branch in the gin and let sit for 24 hours. Remove the branch and discard.

97

98
CIDER BELLINI

THIN RED APPLE SLICE, FOR GARNISH

1 OUNCE APPLE JUICE

1 OUNCE SIMPLE SYRUP (SEE PAGE 9)

½ OUNCE HENNESSY COGNAC

DASH OF GROUND CINNAMON

DASH OF GROUND ALLSPICE

DASH OF GROUND CLOVES

3 TO 4 OUNCES CHAMPAGNE

Place a red apple slice in a champagne flute, and set aside. Combine the apple juice, simple syrup, cognac, cinnamon, allspice, and cloves in a cocktail shaker with ice. Shake vigorously, and strain into the champagne flute over the red apple slice. Top off with the champagne.

99
Spiced Pear Tartini

SIMPLE SYRUP (SEE PAGE 9), FOR MARTINI RIM

CINNAMON-SUGAR MIX, FOR MARTINI RIM

PEAR SLICE, FOR GARNISH

1 ½ OUNCES PEAR LIQUEUR

1 OUNCE PEAR NECTAR (CAN BE FOUND IN MOST
   GROCERY STORES)

SPLASH OF TUACA (A SPICED ITALIAN LIQUEUR)

SPLASH OF FRESH LEMON JUICE

1 OUNCE SWEET SPARKLING WINE (E.G.,
   BALLATORE GRAN SPUMANTE)

Wet the rim of a martini glass with simple syrup.
Dip into cinnamon-sugar mix several times to
ensure coverage. Place the pear slice in the
rimmed martini glass and set aside. Combine the
pear liqueur, pear nectar, Tuaca, and lemon juice
in a cocktail shaker with ice. Shake vigorously and
strain into the rimmed martini glass. Top off with
the sparkling wine.

Just Peachy Cosmo

1 SCOOP PEACH SORBET, SOFTENED
1 ½ OUNCES OCEAN SPRAY WHITE CRANBERRY
  PEACH JUICE
1 ½ OUNCES VODKA
½ OUNCE GRAND MARNIER
SPLASH OF FRESH LEMON JUICE
2 OUNCES GRAN SPUMANTE SPARKLING WINE
BASIL LEAF AND/OR PEACH WEDGE, FOR GARNISH

In a cocktail shaker, combine the peach sorbet
(must be soft or even partially melted), white
cranberry and peach juice, vodka, Grand
Marnier, and lemon juice with ice. Shake vigorously, and strain into a chilled martini glass. Top
with sparkling wine. Garnish with a floating basil
leaf and/or a peach wedge.

101

SPARKLING MOCHA TRUFFLE

A great dessert cocktail—it can be served in a 5-ounce martini glass or in 2 shot glasses.

4 TABLESPOONS CHOCOLATE SHAVINGS, FOR
  GARNISH

¾ OUNCE WHITE CRÈME DE CACAO
  (OR AMSTERDAM CHOCOLATE LIQUEUR, IF
  AVAILABLE), PLUS EXTRA FOR MARTINI RIM

¾ OUNCE VANILLA LIQUEUR

SPLASH OF NOCELLO (WALNUT LIQUEUR)

1 OUNCE BALLATORE RED ROSSO SPUMANTE

Wet the rim of a martini glass or shot glasses in white crème de cacao and dip into a plate of chocolate shavings. Set aside. In a cocktail shaker, combine the ¾ ounce white crème de cacao, vanilla liqueur, and Nocello with ice. Shake vigorously. Add the sparkling wine and stir. Strain into glasses.